Business Writing

Career Step, LLC
Phone: 801.489.9393
Toll-Free: 800.246.7837
Fax: 801.491.6645
careerstep.com

This text companion contains a snapshot of the online program content converted to a printed format. Please note that the online training program is constantly changing and improving and is always the source of the most up-to-date information.

Product Number: HG-PR-11-091
Generation Date: March 10, 2011

Table of Contents

Unit 1
Introduction

Before You Start Writing – Introduction

Good writing requires planning. Even if you're just writing a quick e-mail, or a long and important letter, there are a few important things to think about before you start. This unit will discuss some of the quick questions you can ask yourself as you plan your writing.

Unit 2
Before You Start Writing

Getting Started

Begin your writing with planning. Whether you are writing a several-page letter or a quick one-paragraph e-mail, good writing requires planning. The larger your writing project is, the more time you will need to spend on planning.

There are four important things to consider before you begin writing. Answering these questions will help you understand what you want your message to say:

1. What is my **objective**?

   The reason you sit down to write.
   I want to tell the staff about our new parking rules.

2. What is the **key issue** in my message?

   This is what you want people to remember after reading the message.
   All cars must be out of the parking lot by 5 pm on Fridays.

3. Who is my **audience**?

   The audience is everyone who will read the message.
   Attention: Everyone with a parking pass to our parking lot.

4. What is the best way to **deliver** this message?

   Choose a delivery method that will have the desired impact on readers. Common writing formats are e-mails or letters, but you might realize that a phone call or meeting is better. You could also use a paper interoffice memo so people can post it by their desk as a reminder.

Planning your writing

What is my <u>Objective</u>?
The purpose is to _____ so that readers will _____.

What is the <u>Key Issue</u> in my message?
What is the one thing I want readers to remember?

Who is my <u>Audience</u>?
- Who is the primary reader(s)?
- What does the reader need to know about the subject?
- What is the reader's attitude toward the topic?
- How can the message be presented to meet the reader's needs?
- What's in it for the reader?

What is the best way to <u>Deliver</u> this message?
- Is this best delivered in writing (e-mail or letter), or should it be a conversation (phone call or meeting)?
- When does the message need to be delivered?

I. **MATCHING.**
   Match the correct term to the definition.

   1. ____ everyone who will read the message
   2. ____ what people should remember from the message
   3. ____ method of giving the message to readers
   4. ____ the reason for your message

   A. delivery
   B. key issue
   C. objective
   D. audience

What is Your Objective?

What do you hope to accomplish with your writing? Why do you need to sit down and write?

There are many different reasons to sit down and write a message. For example, you might be writing to share information, to persuade others to your point of view, or to bring about action. Each reason requires a different approach to your writing, so it is important to identify the purpose before anything else. It is a good idea to write the objective at the top of the document—this will help you remember the objective as you write.

Here are a few examples of writing objectives:

- To persuade a client to purchase a new product
- To inform employees of a new parking policy
- To ask for information from a coworker

Remember that the purpose is different from the message. For example, if you are writing a marketing letter, the purpose of the document is to persuade clients to buy your new product. But the key issue—what you want people to remember—is that your new product features cutting-edge technology that will improve efficiency.

> **Planning your writing**
>
> **What is my Objective?**
> The purpose is to _____ so that readers will _____.

What is Your Key Issue?

What do you want readers to remember after they've finished reading your document? This is the subject of the message, or the **key issue**.

You should be able to state the key issue in one or two sentences. If you need more than one or two sentences to do this, you are trying to fit too much into one document. Save unrelated topics for another document.

Here are a few examples of key issues in a document:

- Our new industrial dishwasher will increase efficiency and reduce costs.
- Beginning Monday, all cars must be out of the parking lot by 6 p.m. This policy will be in effect until March 21.
- Please provide an updated deadline for the Alco project at the meeting on Thursday.

Once you've identified the key issue, place it near the top of the document. This makes the most important information easily accessible, which is essential for readers who only read the first few lines of the document.

> **Planning your writing**
>
> What is my Objective?
> The purpose is to _____ so that readers will _____.
>
> **What is the Key Issue in my message?**
> What is the one thing I want readers to remember?

All the paragraphs and sentences in your document should support the key issue. Omit topics that are not directly connected to this issue; save them for other documents or communication.

Who is Your Audience?

Your audience will determine what you write and how you write it. Ask yourself these questions to form a clear picture of your audience:

What is in it for your readers? They are investing the time to read your writing: how will they benefit? Share your message in a way that is meaningful to them.

Will more than one person read your message? Take care to identify each reader, down the individual. If readers can be lumped into groups, identify the groups as necessary.

What do they already know, and what do they need to know, about your message? The needs of the audience are most important in your writing. Writing for them will make your message more clear and accessible.

How will they react to your message? Anticipate the reaction your message will receive and adjust the tone of the message accordingly. If you think they will be receptive, be positive, active, and direct. If you think they will be resistant, use passive, positive language. If you think they will be indifferent, be brief, clear, and strong to make your message heard.

> ### Planning your writing
>
> What is my Objective?
> The purpose is to _____ so that readers will _____.
>
> What is the Key Issue in my message?
> What is the one thing I want readers to remember?
>
> **Who is my Audience?**
> - Who is the primary reader(s)?
> - What does the reader need to know about the subject?
> - What is the reader's attitude toward the topic?
> - How can the message be presented to meet the reader's needs?
> - What's in it for the reader?

How do they like to process information, and how can you tailor your message to satisfy these needs? Many people respond to visuals, so graphs and charts are more appealing than a spreadsheet. However, people who understand the numbers more clearly might appreciate the raw numbers instead.

I. FILL IN THE BLANK.
Enter the correct word in the blank provided.

1. If you think your audience will be resistant, use passive, _____ language.

2. The _____ of the audience are most important in your writing.

3. Anticipate the reaction your message will receive and _____ the tone accordingly.

4. Since your readers are investing time to read your writing, consider how they will _____ from it.

5. Many people respond to _____, so graphs and charts may be appealing to them.

What is the Best Way to Deliver Your Message?

Once you know what the content of your message will be, think about the best way to deliver it. Here are a few pros and cons of the most popular delivery formats of communication in business.

E-mail

Pro: E-mail is a very popular form of communication because messages are instant, informal, and inexpensive. A great majority of modern communication occurs in this format.

Con: People can abuse the flexibility of e-mail with unprofessional writing habits, such as neglecting to use capitalized letters or punctuation and using shorthand.

Letter

Pro: Letters are a formal type of business document printed on an organization's stationery, or sent posted on the company's website. Letters can be sent from one person to another. Letters have a professional tone that causes good reader response.

Con: This form of writing is not good for quick messages and takes more time to deliver than e-mails.

Memo

Pro: Memos are a quick and efficient way to communicate within an organization. They can be sent on paper or through e-mail. Organizations usually have a template that employees can fill out when creating a memo. Memos are best for announcements, or quick brief messages.

Con: Because memos are so brief, it's easy for them to be ignored or only skimmed through. The template often limits the amount of information that can be conveyed.

It's important to consider timing when you deliver your message. If timing is an issue, choose a format that's going to get the message there on time.

Planning your writing

What is my <u>Objective</u>?
The purpose is to _____ so that readers will _____.

What is the <u>Key Issue</u> in my message?
What is the one thing I want readers to remember?

Who is my <u>Audience</u>?
- Who is the primary reader(s)?
- What does the reader need to know about the subject?
- What is the reader's attitude toward the topic?
- How can the message be presented to meet the reader's needs?
- What's in it for the reader?

What is the best way to <u>Deliver</u> this message?
- Is this best delivered in writing (e-mail or letter), or should it be a conversation (phone call or meeting)?
- When does the message need to be delivered?

While e-mail is a quick, easy, and common form of communication, it is not always the best way to communicate. Sometimes a phone call or a meeting would be more effective.

	Pros	Cons
E-mail	• Instant communication • Best for short, quick messages • Flexible format, messages can be formal or informal and additional information can be attached • Inexpensive to deliver • Recipients can read messages anytime, from anywhere • Can communicate to make people with one message • Many people use email as their primary form of business communication • Easy to store and file	• Messages can be misunderstood • Writers use bad habits in e-mail (no capitalized letters or punctuation, text message shorthand) • Messages can be ignored or simply missed among other messages • Spam filters may filter out messages • Communication is on record and can be referenced later
Letter	• Formal communication • Can communicate to many people	• Take more time to write and deliver • Harder to store and file
Memo	• Quick communication • Great for announcements and brief messages • Memo forms make communication easy to facilitate	• Messages are very brief • Only for interoffice communication

I. MULTIPLE CHOICE.
Choose the correct delivery message that each pro and con is describing.

1. Con: not good for quick messages.
   ○ E-mail
   ○ Letter
   ○ Memo

2. Pro: can be sent on paper or through e-mail.
   ○ E-mail
   ○ Letter
   ○ Memo

3. Con: unprofessional writing occurs.
   ○ E-mail
   ○ Letter
   ○ Memo

4. Pro: may serve as interoffice communication to the entire office.

○ E-mail
○ Letter
○ Memo

5. Con: shorthand and neglect of capitalization happens.

○ E-mail
○ Letter
○ Memo

Unit 3
What to Say and How to Say It

What to Say and How to Say It – Introduction

Write out your document once you have gone through the planning process and you know what your message needs to include. The key to making this step of the process successful is remembering that you must write out everything before you start to edit and pare down. Don't edit your words as they come to mind. Instead, write everything out first, then go back and edit. You will learn more about how to create a first rough draft in this unit.

After you have your thoughts and an idea of what you want to say, it may be difficult to get your words to sound right. How do you shape your words so that they convey not only the information you want to share, but also the right emotion and tone? The second half of this unit shares writing techniques and words you can use to give your documents the right tone.

Getting Your Thoughts Organized

It is very helpful to get your thoughts organized before you start writing. Mainly, this involves identifying the supporting points of the key issue, and deciding their order of importance. Some documents are short enough that knowing the purpose, audience, and key issue are enough to begin writing. But others that are longer and take more time may require additional planning. If you want additional help getting organized and getting your thoughts in order, try one of these start-up methods.

Outlining

Some of us remember this process from writing classes in high school. This helps you organize and identify the main topics and supporting points in a document.

> **Outlining**
>
> I. Advertise position opening
>   A. Newspaper
>   B. Web site
>   1. Our site
>   2. Job sites
>   a. CareerBuilder
>   b. Monster
>   c. Jobs.com
> II. Choose top applicants
>   A. Look for lots of related experience
>   B. Diverse background

Answer the Five W's (and One H)

Ask yourself who, what, why, where, when, and how. This method answers readers' questions before they come up. Be very specific when answering your questions.

Question: When is the meeting?
Vague: The meeting will be next week.
Specific: The meeting will be on Thursday, July 17th at 10:30 am.

Five W's

<u>What</u> is this message about? The new project manager.
<u>Who</u> is the new employee? Reed Stephens
<u>When</u> will he start? He will start on Monday, March 16
<u>Why</u> was he hired? He was hired to help us meet our new production demands.
<u>Where</u> is his desk? His office is next to the conference room.
<u>How</u> can we contact him? Ext. 7003

Brainstorming

Write down topics and thoughts as they come up, drawing connections as they appear. This free-form thought process helps identify connection between topics.

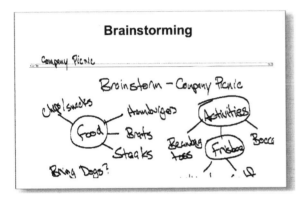

Freewriting

Write thoughts as they enter your mind, and keep writing, even if your thoughts don't pertain to the document you are trying to write. This is another free process that helps you get "unstuck" in your writing.

Freewriting

I am writing to let you know about the bad experience I had at your restaurant. I wanted to order the ribs but the hamburger looked better on the menu. The waiter recommended the hamburger too. I wonder if more people get hamburgers than ribs? The hamburger wasn't very good, so I wish I had ordered the ribs. The sides weren't very good either. The mashed

I. TRUE/FALSE.
Mark the following true or false.

1. Outlining is when you write down topics and thoughts as they come up, drawing connections as they appear.
   - ◯ true
   - ◯ false

2. Writing thoughts as they enter your mind, even if they don't pertain to the document you are trying to write, is called freewriting.
   - ◯ true
   - ◯ false

3. Brainstorming includes the five W's.
   - ◯ true
   - ◯ false

Anatomy of Communication

All communication—whether written or spoken—has three basic parts: a greeting, a discussion or body, and a closing. Each part has a role in conveying and communicating a message. Use this basic structure as a guideline when you write your business documents.

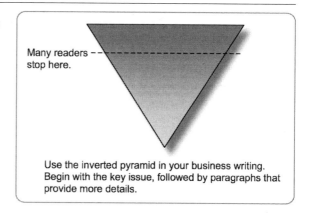

Use the inverted pyramid in your business writing. Begin with the key issue, followed by paragraphs that provide more details.

Greeting

The greeting is where communication begins. This is where the tone is set, and readers learn what to expect from the rest of the document. Be sure to structure your document so that readers don't need to read past the greeting to get the most important information. The greeting serves two purposes:

- State the key issue of the document.
- Set the tone for the document.

Body

The body is where the bulk of information and communication takes place. Each paragraph in the body should be directly connected to the key issue. The body is where the supporting points of the key issue are shared, and where persuasion takes place.

Closing

The closing of a document is where the communication ends and you can leave a last impression. The closing serves three purposes:

1. A summary repeats the key issue and reminds readers if action is required.
2. A closing statement leaves the last impression on the reader. Close the document with a statement that reflects the tone of the greeting.
3. A signature identifies who the message is from. Many organizations have a policy on how signatures should appear in documents.

Dear Howie,

Congratulations on your promotion!

Rayna Oden told me the good news last week. I understand you were chosen from a large pool of candidates; what a great testament to your skills and talents as a programmer.

I look forward to working with you more in the near future.

Sincerely,

Reed Stephens

Reed Stephens
Project Manager

I. FILL IN THE BLANK.
Enter the correct word in the blank provided.

1. All communication has three basic parts: a greeting, a discussion or _____, and a closing.

2. A _____ repeats the key issue and reminds readers if action is required.

3. The two purposes of a greeting are to state the key issue and _____ for the document.

4. Each paragraph in the body should be directly connected to the _____.

Writing Paragraphs and Sentences

The bulk of your writing occurs in the body of the document, where you provide the information that supports the key issue. This lesson discusses some basic rules to remember as you write out your documents.

Building with paragraphs

A paragraph is a unit of writing that supports the key issue. A paragraph may be long or short, depending on the amount of information you want to communicate. Here are a few guidelines for paragraph structure:

Subject	Verb	Object

The admin prints the letter.

The harried and busy admin prints the long and important letter.

Harried and busy, the admin prints the letter.

- Start each paragraph with a topic sentence. This makes your writing easy to scan and it signals development of the key issue.
- Each paragraph sentence supports the topic sentence. This keeps related information together, and helps to weed out unnecessary sentences.
- Keep paragraphs to five sentences or less. People do not want to read paragraphs that are longer than this. If you have a long paragraph, divide it into two paragraphs, or edit out unnecessary information.

Writing sentences

Sentences communicate your thoughts, so it is important that they are clear and easy to understand. Here are a few rules for sentence composition:

- Use the Subject Verb Object (SVO) structure for simple, clear sentences. The most direct and clear way to build your sentences is to use the SVO sentence structure. Begin with the Subject, the person or thing the sentence is about; the Verb, the action that the subject is doing; and the Object, the person or thing receiving the action.
- Vary sentence structure. While the SVO sentence structure is the clearest way to organize sentences, using only this structure will make your writing sound stilted and monotonous. Make your writing flow by varying the structure. For example, combine two sentences into one, include additional clauses in a sentence, and place words of emphasis at the beginning or end of the sentence.

Stilted writing
The admin prints the letter. The printer hums when it warms up the ink. The paper comes out. The letter is folded and inserted into an envelope. The letter is sent.

Varied structure
The admin prints the letter and the printer hums as it warms up the ink. After the paper comes out, the letter is folded, inserted into an envelope, and sent.

Concern yourself with getting it written before you worry about getting it right. Ultimately, use your ear to guide you. Your writing should express your thoughts.

I. MULTIPLE CHOICE.
Choose the best answer.

1. Which of the following is NOT true about a paragraph?
   - ○ A paragraph supports the key issue.
   - ○ Each paragraph contains only one subject, verb, and object.
   - ○ A paragraph may be long or short.
   - ○ Each paragraph should begin with a topic sentence.

2. The subject is _____.
   - ○ the action
   - ○ the person or thing receiving the action
   - ○ the person or thing
   - ○ the word that describes the verb

3. Which of the following is a way to vary your sentence structure?
   - ○ Combine two sentences into one.
   - ○ Include additional clauses in a sentence.
   - ○ Place words of emphasis at the beginning of a sentence.
   - ○ You can do any of the above to vary the structure of a sentence.

Write the Right Way

Have you given up on writing? Do you think that writing is a skill you either have or you don't? Or maybe do you think that writing isn't part of your job? Writing is something that anyone can do well, and it's also something that most everyone uses in their job. E-mails, messages, memos, letters; they all involve writing. Anyone can become a good writer with a good process to guide them, practice, and time.

Good writing is essential in successful business. Writing is an important form of communication, and good communication establishes a foundation of trust and collaboration between everyone you work with, such as coworkers, business associates, and customers. Your writing tells other people a lot about your personality and your intellect. An organized, thoughtful document with supporting points suggests thinking that is insightful and clear. On the other hand, a disorganized, error-laden document suggests thinking that is hasty and careless. Follow these basic but valuable rules so ensure your business writing leaves a positive impression:

Be Concise: Use only the words that are necessary to convey your message.

Be Clear: Be specific instead of general, definite instead of vague, and concrete instead of abstract.

Be Active: The active voice is concise and direct, and it has an energetic and confident quality.

Be Positive: This style of writing is easy to read, makes definite statements, and avoids hesitating and noncommittal language.

Be Professional: When you are professional, you act in a way that meets the standards of your profession.

Be Yourself: Your writing should reflect your personality and your emotional response to the subject of your message.

> ### Why Write the Right Way?
>
> ✓ Good communicators are successful at advancing their careers.
>
> ✓ Quality business writing inspires confidence in customers, co-workers, and other business partners.
>
> ✓ Clear communication makes it possible to direct others to action, persuade others to your point of view, and share important information.

I. TRUE/FALSE.
Mark the following true or false.

1. To be concise is to use only words that are necessary to convey your message.
   - ◯ true
   - ◯ false

2. To be professional is to use a concise and direct voice with energetic and confident quality.
   - ◯ true
   - ◯ false

3. To be positive is to act in a way that meets the standards of your profession.
   - ◯ true
   - ◯ false

4. To be yourself is to use writing that reflects your personality.
   - ◯ true
   - ◯ false

5. To be active is to be specific instead of general.
   - ◯ true
   - ◯ false

Be Concise

To be concise is to omit needless words. This does not mean that all your sentences should be short or that all your details should be left out; it means eliminating unnecessary words and information.

Avoid redundancy

Redundancy occurs when you use words with the same meaning, and by writing sentences with the same information. Replace redundant phrases with one word, and remove statements of the same information.

My personal opinion is that our best days are ahead.
My opinion is that our best days are ahead.

Use fewer words

Many common phrases are wordy. For example, "there is no doubt that" has the same meaning as "no doubt." Using fewer words adds impact to a sentence.

There is no doubt that the merger will be contentious.
No doubt the merger will be contentious.

Wordy and Redundant

For all intents and purposes, the report from the first quarter predicted the future financial results to play out in the second quarter. In my humble opinion, I think the precipitous drops in profits, and the exponential increases in expenses, are perfect conditions for a company saving and resource combining merger.

Concise

The first quarter report predicted the financial results of the second quarter. The drops in profits and increases in expenses make perfect conditions for a merger.

Wordy	Concise
on account of the fact that	because
at a later date	later
in spite of the fact that	although
perform an analysis of	analyze
pertaining to	about
at your earliest convenience	soon *or* by X date
as soon as	when
a majority of	most
along the lines of	like
for the purpose of	for
in the near future	soon
the reason why is that	because
he is a man who	he is
made a decision	decide

Redundant	Concise
goals and objectives	goals
one and the same	the same
past experience	experience
free gift	gift
current status	status
enter into	enter
any and all	all
check into	check
whether or not	whether
absolutely perfect	perfect
this particular instance	this instance
advance planning	advance
close proximity	near
past history	past

Be Clear

Clear writing calls up pictures, making your message easy to understand and remember. Be specific instead of general, definite instead of vague, and concrete instead of abstract. Do not expect readers to read between the lines, or to infer meaning from veiled references.

Be specific

Unless the nature of your document requires you to be vague, be as specific as possible.

Vague: I need you to make good progress today.

Specific: I need the *Go Green* account to be completed by 5:00 pm today.

Use simple words

Large words can cloud your message and make you sound pretentious. Simple words make your meaning clear.

Overblown: Implementation of reorganization procedures with the intent to downsize are anticipated to begin in the near future.

Simple: We will begin cutbacks in the near future.

Do not hedge

Avoid using passive filler words because you do not know what to say, or because you fear others will disagree with you. These words do not add meaning; they only weaken your message.

Hedging: For all intents and purposes, the design was pretty much wrapped up before the editors gave input.

Clear: The design was wrapped up before the editors gave input.

Avoid jargon and acronyms

Jargon and acronyms should only be used if the audience is familiar with them: if nine out of ten readers are familiar with the jargon or acronym, you may use it. Otherwise, write out the acronym the first time it is referenced, then use the acronym in the rest of the document. For example, you could write this: "The Securities and Exchange Commission (SEC) has published their annual report. You may view the report on the SEC website."

Unclear

It has recently come to management's attention that unidentified individuals are purportedly consuming mid-day meals that belong to others from the dining facility's cold-storage repository.

Clear

Someone has been stealing lunches from the break-room refrigerator.

Overblown	Simple
advise	tell
ascertain	find out
demonstrate	show
duplicate	copy
indicate	show
initiate	being
obtain	get
orientate	orient
terminate	end, fire
utilize	use

Hedging words and phrases	
pretty	it is considered to be
probably	practically
I would guess that	somewhat
for the most part	very
rather	virtually

Clichés and tired phrases	
state of the art	please be advised that
beyond the shadow of a doubt	permit me to say
last but not least	it has been deemed necessary

Avoid cliches

Cliches and overused phrases make your message sound trite, tired, and unspecific. Avoid them like the plague.

I. FILL IN THE BLANK.
Enter the correct word in the blank provided.

1. Be specific instead of general, _____ instead of vague.

2. Avoid using _____ words because you don't know what to say.

3. Jargon and _____ should only be used if the audience is familiar with them.

Be Active

Normally, you will want to use the active voice to more clearly get a point across to your readers. However, there is also a time and a place for the passive voice. The active voice helps the reader picture what is happening. The passive voice is more difficult to envision.

> **Use action verbs to convey good news.**
>
> **Passive:** The Sales Associate of the Year award *was won* by Dinah.
>
> **Active:** Dinah *won* the Sales Associate of the Year award.

Active writing

The active voice is concise and direct, and it has an energetic and confident quality. In active sentences, the subject does the action.

Active: Chris will prepare the agenda.

Passive: The agenda will be prepared by Chris.

In the active example, you can picture Chris sitting down to prepare the agenda. In the passive example, it is more difficult to picture the agenda receiving the action. The active voice makes sentences that are strong and brief, while passive voice makes sentences weak and dull.

Active: Ice buildup caused the power lines to break.

Passive: The reason the power went out was that ice buildup broke the lines.

Passive writing

While passive writing is discouraged, it definitely has a place in your documents. Use it when:

You want to focus on the action, not the actor.

- Kitty was rewarded with an extra vacation day. (The focus is on Kitty, instead of the extra vacation day.)
- The zoo was built in 1982. (The focus is on the zoo, not its builders.)
- The settings on the network were changed. (The focus is on the network settings, not the person who changed them.)

You want to hide something or do not want to come across as harsh.

- Bonuses have been approved. (The people approving the bonuses are left out.)
- The steak was burned. (The focus is on the steak, not who burned it.)

I. MATCHING.
Determine whether the following sentences are active or passive voice.

1. ____ The CEO requested a meeting in the boardroom.

2. ____ The e-mail was sent by John.

3. ____ I took an hour-long lunch break today.

4. ____ Health benefits have been lowered since last year.

5. ____ The letter was given to the administrative assistant to review.

A. active
B. passive

Be Positive

It's good business to be positive. Success in business is influenced by positive interactions and experiences. Therefore, business writing should be positive whenever possible. The positive form of writing is easy to read, and it creates goodwill with the reader so your message is more likely to appeal to your audience. Positive writing reaches people on a subconscious level. People want to know what is, rather than what is not. Negative statements make people feel caged in and discouraged. Positives make people feel guided and encouraged.

Make positive statements

You can make a stronger statement by avoiding the word not, which makes your sentences ambiguous and weak.

Express negatives in positive form.
    She **did not think** that data entry was **important**.
    She thought data entry was **unimportant**.

Negative words other than *not* are strong.
    I **did not** know she was so talented.
    I **never** knew she was so talented.

Conditional words, such as *could, would, should, may,* and *can* are indefinite. Reserve them for expressing uncertainty.
    I **would** be happy to assist with the audit.
    I **will** be happy to assist with the audit.

State ideas positively rather than negatively.

Negative: Don't leave the lights on when you leave a room.

Positive: Please remember to turn off the lights when you leave a room.

Negative: I hope you're not disappointed with the presentation.

Positive: I hope you have enjoyed the presentation.

When writing a complimentary or congratulatory message, use specific language to make the message even more positive.

Vague: The sales department did a great job this week.

Specific: Congratulations to George, Maya, and Terry for bringing in six new clients this week!

Communicating criticism

Be cautious with your style and tone when communicating criticism. While you need to present bad news in the best possible light, you must also be honest. Here are two ways to soften criticism:

1. Sandwich a negative between positives.
   You did a great job processing the Satellite Energy case. Our client was very pleased. Next time, please document your steps more thoroughly. Our admin had trouble following the paperwork. Overall, you handled the customer's concerns superbly—what a great way to begin your caseload.
2. Use passive verbs and courteous modifiers to make a criticism more polite.

Harsh: Stop surfing the Internet during office hours and get your work done.

Polite: Please stay off the Internet during office hours so you can stay focused on work-related projects.

> **Avoid ruining a compliment by tacking on a criticism.**
>
> Felicia's exceptional debating skills won the Brown case, even though she was very late to the negotiations.
>
> (The compliment is lost because the last words were critical.)

Be Professional

When you are professional, you act in a way that meets the standards of your profession, such as being courteous and respectful of peers and other business associates. To be professional, keep the message focused on the subject at hand. This is especially important when communicating messages that could evoke an emotional reaction. It is especially important to keep your message free of politics, religion, and gender.

Politics

Everyone is entitled to their own opinion on politics. Politics is a hot-button issue, so don't bring it up in writing or conversation. Political campaigns are the only place where politics is appropriate.

Religion

Like politics, everyone is entitled to their own religious beliefs. You may not discriminate according to these beliefs. The holiday season is one time where a religious acknowledgement may be appropriate—such as "Merry Christmas"—although you might be best off wishing people "Happy Holidays" to include the many different celebrations that happen during that time of the year.

Gender

The key to avoiding sexist language is to be sensitive to your reader by being aware of the hidden or overt meanings of things. If you write, "Thanks to all the salesmen who helped us reach our sales goal!" the women on your sales team are left out. Write "sales reps" or "salespeople" and everyone is included in the compliment.

> **Use gender neutral job titles:**
>
> | Gender neutral | Gender biased |
> | --- | --- |
> | letter carrier | postman |
> | meteorologist | weatherman |
> | police officer | policeman |
> | reporter | newsman |
> | chair | chairman |
> | flight attendant | steward/stewardess |
> | server | waiter/waitress |

When a person writes an e-mail, *he* should be careful to remain gender neutral.

Repeat the noun. When a person writes an e-mail, *the person* should be careful to remain gender neutral.

Rewrite the sentence as plural. When *people* writes e-mails, *they* should be careful to remain gender neutral.

Use the phrase "he or she." When a person writes an e-mail, *he or she* should be careful to remain gender neutral.

Use the generic pronoun "one." When *one* writes an e-mail, *one* should be careful to remain gender neutral.

Reword the sentence. When writing e-mail, a person should be careful to remain gender neutral.

I. **MATCHING.**
    Determine whether the following job titles are gender neutral or gender biased

1. ____ police officer
2. ____ waitress
3. ____ chair
4. ____ reporter
5. ____ weatherman
6. ____ server
7. ____ postman
8. ____ stewardess

A. gender neutral
B. gender biased

Be Yourself

Your writing is an expression of you. It should reflect your personality and your emotional response to the subject of your message.

Write the way you speak

Imagine you are talking to a friend as you write. This will help you avoid awkward and unclear language, and instead use words and phrases that come easily to you. It will also help you concentrate on the subject so you don't have to worry about how you sound. Honesty and simplicity will shine through.

Stiff and stilted

Dear Ms. Trudeau:

I am writing to express gratitude for your willingness to assist me with my presentation yesterday. The data was more than sufficient for my needs.

Please notify me when I can return the favor in kind.

Sincerely,
James

Be relaxed

Unless the circumstances of your document require formality, make your writing as conversational as you can. Your readers will respond better if they feel you are relaxed and pleasant in your writing.

Focus on the subject

Content is most important; your temper and mood will come through as you focus on the key topic.

Be honest

Writing is an expression of you. Use the words or phrases that come easily to you. Being honest with yourself allows you to express the message clearly.

Relaxed and conversational

Dear Jeanne,

Thanks so much for helping me out with the presentation yesterday. The data you provided was easy to read and it supported my arguments very well.

Let me know when I can return the favor!

Thanks,
James

Highlights

Tips for being yourself:

- Writing works best when it sounds like a real person talking to real people.
- Write in a conversational style. Lofty, overblown language gives the impression that you are trying to be more important than you are.
- Don't be afraid to use "I." It connects readers with a real person.
- "Being yourself" does not mean you should declare your emotion or mood as it relates to the subject. Let this be revealed in the way you communicate your message.

Good Writing Checklist

Follow this quick summary of writing guidelines for a refresher on good writing.

☑ Be concise

    Avoid redundancy: My personal opinion has the same meaning as My opinion.

    Use fewer words: There is no doubt that has the same meaning as No doubt.

☑ Be clear

    Be specific: Do this later today is not as specific as Do this by 2 p.m. today.

    Use simple words: Initiate the untilization of is not as clear as Begin to use.

    Do not hedge: I would guess that it is done soon is not as clear as It is done soon.

Avoid jargon and acronyms: If you use an acronym, write it out the first time it is used.

Avoid clichés: Clichés and overused phrases make your message tired and unspecific.

☑ Be active

Write energetically: Be confident in your writing.

Make the subject do the action: <u>I picked up the pen</u> instead of <u>The pen was picked up by me</u>.

☑ Be positive

Make positive statements: Avoid "not": <u>unimportant</u> is more positive than <u>not important</u>.

Communicate criticism positively: Sandwich a negative between positives or use passive language.

☑ Be professional

Politics: Political campaigns are the only place where politics is appropriate.

Religion: Avoid religion: "Happy Holidays" is okay during the holiday season.

Gender: Be sensitive to what you say: "Thanks to our salesmen!" leaves out the women on your sales team.

☑ Be yourself

Write the way you speak: Imagine you are talking to a friend, writing words that come easily.

Be relaxed: Make your writing as conversational as you can.

Focus on the subject: Your temper and mood will come through as you focus on the key topic.

Be honest: Writing is an expression of you. Being honest with yourself allows you to express the message clearly.

Unit 4
Editing and Design

Editing and Design – Introduction

Now the hard work begins. Editing is difficult because after all the work of writing, you're reluctant to cut it away. Unfortunately, that's the purpose of editing, to shape your message so it is clear, sharp, and clean, even if it means getting messy and hacking away the unrelated parts first. Editing is the most important process of your writing. Don't skip it or ignore it. Take the time to sculpt the words and phrases you've used into a more clear and refined message—and get rid of distracting and clunky errors.

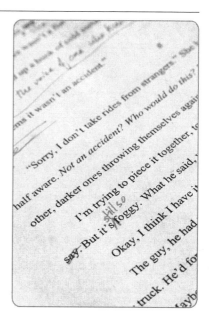

After you read about editing in this unit, we'll discuss document design. The words in your document are the most important parts of your message. They will definitely take the bulk of your time in the writing of a document. However, the design of a document is a convincing factor in whether readers choose to read the document in the first place. This unit talks about design strategies that make your document appealing to your audience, such as visual aids and formatting that make the document reader-friendly. Here we go!

Preparing to Edit

Revising your work is essential in writing: rarely will you get the message right in the first draft. Read through your work and revise it until it says what you really want it to say. Here are a few things you can do to prepare your eyes and your mind for editing.

Step away before you dig in

If time allows, give yourself some time away from the document. Get a drink of water, go to your lunch break, or leave the document until the next day. Give yourself time away from your writing so you have a fresh perspective and a sharp eye for editing.

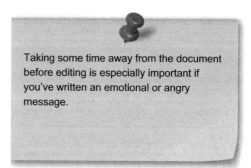

Taking some time away from the document before editing is especially important if you've written an emotional or angry message.

Get feedback from others

Sharing your writing with others is a great way to make sure your document reads the way you want it to. Ask for feedback on the document, such as:

1. What is the key issue?
2. What are questions that come up while reading the document?
3. How is the tone of the message?

Gathering feedback from other people before sending the message is especially useful if you are writing a document that has bad news. Then, edit the document yourself to make sure it represents you well. An insightful, organized, and error-free document gives readers the impression that you are insightful, organized, and detail-oriented.

Print the document

No matter how accustomed you are to reading and writing on the computer screen, it is still easier to read from paper. Proofreading a hardcopy will help you see errors you might miss on a computer screen. It also gives you a better sense of how the document flows.

Check the document design

Make sure the document is easy to scan and is clearly organized. Check for such things as white space, alignment, and paragraph and sentence length. If the document is long, add headings to help direct the reader and organize content.

Read the document aloud

Hearing your message will give you a better idea of how it will sound to others as they read it. It also helps to catch errors you might miss while silently reading, such as missing words or misspellings.

I. FILL IN THE BLANK.
Enter the correct word in the blank provided.

1. When checking document design, it is important to check for things like _____, alignment, and paragraph and sentence length.

2. Reading the document aloud helps catch errors you might miss while _____ reading.

3. Taking time away from the document before editing is especially important if you've written an emotional or _____ message.

4. Asking for _____ from others is a great way to make sure your document reads the way you want it to.

Editing Checklist

It is important to edit your document before sending it out. Whether it is a short e-mail to a co-worker you speak to often, or a letter that you're sending to an important client, your writing represents you and your ability to communicate and think clearly. Take the time to edit your document and represent yourself well.

Editing your document is like checking yourself in the mirror one last time before you go out: make sure you don't have any spinach in your teeth.

Proofreading

Even the best of writers make errors from time to time. Use this checklist to make sure your document is accurate and error free.

Proofreading checklist	
Names, titles, and company names	Make sure all the names and titles of people and names of companies are correctly spelled and worded.
Dates	Double check dates against a calendar. For example, if you write *Wednesday, February 11*, make sure February 11 is a Wednesday.
Numbers and statistics	Are the numbers and amounts correct? Do you want to spend $5,525 or $2,252?

Misused words	This happens often with words that sound the same but spellings and meanings are different. For example, you spend *capital* and you go to the *capitol*.
Repeated words	It can be easy to miss repeated words, especially when they fall on a line break: *"She was was the nominee in the school election."* Fortunately, most word processor and e-mail programs highlight repeated words. Even if the use of repeated words is grammatically correct, it is wiser to rephrase the sentence. "He let her know that chocolate was what he wanted," is much easier to read than, "He let her know that that was what he wanted."
Small words	Small words can be easy to miss because you tend to read what you expect to see. For example, find the missing *as* in this sentence: "Use your eyes as well your computer tools."
Acronyms and jargon	Acronyms and jargon should only be used if you are certain the audience is familiar with them. If you must use acronyms, write out the full name with the acronym the first time it is referenced, as in "Securities and Exchange Commission (SEC)." You may use the acronym after it has been defined in the document.
Word or phrase abbreviations	Abbreviations—such as IMHO (in my humble opinion), LOL (laughing out loud), and l8r (later)—are inappropriate for business writing. Reserve them for personal communication in texts, e-mails, and instant messages.
Use electronic tools	Word processors and e-mail programs are equipped with tools that check your documents for errors, such as typos and misspellings. Use these whenever possible, but don't rely on them completely; they can't correct meaning. For example, "He will not accept the settlement," has a much different meaning than, "He will now accept the settlement."

Editing

You've proofread the document and have corrected the typos and misspellings. Now use this checklist to make sure it says what you want it to say.

Editing checklist	
Key issue is clear and concise, and is clearly included at the beginning of the document.	The key issue is the most important part of the document. Readers should be able to read the key issue and know exactly what the document is about.
Design is easy to read and is inviting to the reader.	Consider all of these aspects in the document design: white space; bulleted and numbered list; 5–7 line paragraphs; and visual elements, including pictures, tables, and fonts.
Writing is correct, clear, and concise.	The facts, numbers, and statistics are correct and words and descriptions are clear and concrete. The language omits needless words.
Supporting points are directly related to the issue.	All the paragraphs in the document should be connected to the key issue, and should move the message or argument of the document forward.
Action required of the reader is clearly stated.	If you want the reader to do something, clearly state the action near the beginning of the document. Repeat the request at the end in long documents.

Writing style is active, positive, and professional	This style of business writing focuses on the information you want to communicate with your reader.
Writing reflects me.	Does the writing reflect you positively? Is it relaxed, honest, and sincere? Will the readers see you in your writing?

Font Formatting

A font is a set of characters with the same design and shape. Formatting document fonts gives your documents greater impact and makes them easier to read. The font type of a document says a lot about the look and feel of a document. For example, a professional document would probably use a more formal font like

Times New Roman. On the other hand, a more

informal document might use the playful Curlz font.

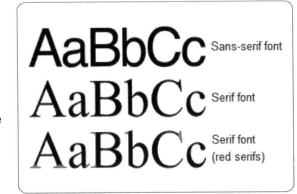

Sans-serif font

Serif font

Serif font (red serifs)

Font type

There are two categories of font types: serif and sans serif.

> **Serif:** Serifs are the details at the ends of letters and symbols. Serif typefaces are considered easier to read in the body text of printed documents.

> **Sans serif:** A sans serif typeface does not have serifs at the ends of letters. Sans serif typefaces are used in headlines, headings, and short documents with a casual feel. Sans serif typefaces are often used for text read on a computer screen.

Common Font Types	
Serif	**Sans serif**
Times New Roman	Arial
Garamond	Verdana
Courier	Trebuchet MS
BODONI	Calibri

Font size

The font size controls how large or small the characters appear to be. The number one rule with font size is visibility: text should always to be easy to see.

Common Font Sizes	
10 point	Large amounts of text
12 point	Large amounts of text
14 point	Subheadings, headings, titles
18 point	Headings, titles

Bold vs. Italics

Within a larger body of text, a piece in *italics* does not stand out much; instead, it signifies a context difference only *while* the text is being read. By contrast, a single word in **boldface** attracts the human eye and is therefore recommended for **keywords** for which the reader is looking.

Font effects

You can emphasize text in a document by adding **bold** and *italic* font effects.

Bold: Boldface emphasizes text by making it darker than surrounding text. Words in boldface strongly stand out from the rest; use boldface to make keywords easily visible for scanning.

Italic: Italics emphasizes text by displaying the font in script style. Text in italics does not stick out much from the rest of the text. It is usually used to mark passages of a different context, such as words from foreign languages or book titles.

I. **TRUE/FALSE.**
   Mark the following true or false.

1. A sans serif typeface includes the details at the end of letters and symbols.
   ○ true
   ○ false

2. Boldface emphasizes text by making it darker than surrounding text.
   ○ true
   ○ false

3. A font is a set of characters with the same design and shape.
   ○ true
   ○ false

Paragraph Formatting

Paragraphs organize the topics that support the key issue of the document. Formatting gives visual signals to the reader so they can easily find information among paragraphs.

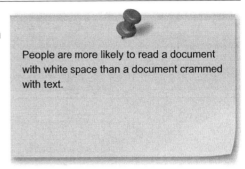

People are more likely to read a document with white space than a document crammed with text.

White space

White space is one of the best ways to make a document look inviting to a reader. White space is restful for the eye, it gives the impression that the document is easy to read, and it makes information easy to find. There are several ways you can design white space into your document.

Write short paragraphs. Keep paragraphs to around five sentences, or five to seven lines. This will keep you from accumulating long, intimidating blocks of text.

Increase the spacing between paragraphs. Use a blank space to indicate a break between paragraphs.

Use margins. Margins provide a frame of white space around the text and visual elements of a document. Use margins of at least one inch in your documents.

White space can give a page a classic, elegant, or rich appearance.

Documents without much white space look cluttered and difficult to read.

Lists

Lists draw attention to important items and are easy to scan. There are two types of lists that people typically use: bulleted and numbered.

Bulleted lists are useful for information that does not need to be presented in a particular order; list items are equal. Bullets highlight important information, and they let you summarize a thought into a short phrase.

Numbered lists are useful for information that is presented in order.

Bulleted list	Numbered list
There are several reasons we should use Metro Sales as our copy machine provider: • They take care of maintenance and tech support issues. • Copy machines are replaced every two years. • Laser printers can be bundled at a discount. • Cost is only slightly higher than if we buy.	Here instructions for making coffee: 1. Dump out the old coffee grounds. 2. Place a new filter in the tray and pour 6 scoops of coffee grounds into the filter. 3. Fill the carafe with cold water to line 12. 4. Pour the water into the coffee reservoir. 5. Turn the machine on.

I. MULTIPLE CHOICE.
Choose the best answer.

1. Keep paragraphs to around (○ five, ○ ten) sentences.

2. (○ Bulleted, ○ Numbered) lists are useful for information that is presented in order.

3. To provide a frame of white space around the text and visual elements of a document, you would adjust the (○ paragraphs, ○ margins).

4. (○ White space, ○ A margin) is restful for the eye.

Tips for Formatting

Font formatting tips

- Keep content to one page. People are more likely to read the document if they can see that the document isn't very long.
- Body text should always be 10 points or larger. Headings within a document should be larger than the body text so that they stand out.
- Use standard system fonts that everyone has when you share documents via e-mail or a network, such as Times New Roman, Arial, Garamond, and Verdana.
- Use no more than two fonts in a document: one for headings and another for the body. A third may be used for extra items, such as headers and footers, or a cover page.
- Headings should appear in bold and in a font type that is different from the body.
- Use font effects to make important points stand out, such as bold, underline, or font color.
- Sans serif fonts are best for documents read on a screen, such as e-mail messages or documents shared electronically.
- Serif fonts are best for printed documents. They also are more elegant than sans serif fonts.

Marketing meeting
Recent changes in our economy have created an opportunity for us to increase business with consumers. We will discuss how to change our marketing message to take advantage of this opportunity at a meeting on **Thursday, November 26** at **9:30 a.m.** in the **conference room**. Everyone is required to attend. Please mark this on your calendars.

We will discuss these issues at the meeting:

- How can we get the attention of more people in the consumer market?
- Which of our products are enticing to consumers?
- What branding initiatives can we focus on to set us apart from competitors?

MVP: Marketing consultants
MVP is a marketing firm that we have hired to help us with our message. The team we have been working with will join the meeting via conference call.

Questions?
Contact Al Newman, our marketing manager, with questions or suggestions for this meeting or marketing in general.

Paragraph formatting tips

- Use paragraph spacing to create white space between paragraphs instead of pressing ENTER.
- Keep lists short. If lists are really long, nothing will stand out.

Tables

A table is a grid of rows and columns that creates cells where you can place text or numbers. Tables are a great way to present information and complex data. Facts, statistics, and large amounts of related information are suitable for tables.

The key to using tables effectively is formatting and designing them in a very readable way. Here are a few tips you can follow to design your tables well:

Include a table title. This makes it easy to reference the table in the text of the document.

Use row and column headings to label data. These headings show the readers how to read the data.

Use lines and shading to mark rows and columns. Lines and shading set rows and columns apart from each other, making them easier to read.

Hide lines to show organized information. You may also hide the lines of a table to show the information in an organized manner.

Year 20XX	Q1	Q2	Q3	Q4
Flights	$15,000	$16,000	$15,000	$16,000
Tour Packages	$28,000	$23,000	$25,000	$22,000
Cruises	$5,000	$5,000	$4,000	$8,000
Other Income	$500	$500	$500	$500
Total	**$48,500**	**$44,500**	**$44,500**	**$46,500**

Tables are used to show data in an organized way. This data is shown in a table with hidden lines…

Year 20XX	Q1	Q2	Q3	Q4
Flights	$15,000	$16,000	$15,000	$16,000
Tour Packages	$28,000	$23,000	$25,000	$22,000
Cruises	$5,000	$5,000	$4,000	$8,000
Other Income	$500	$500	$500	$500
Total	**$48,500**	**$44,500**	**$44,500**	**$46,500**

…While the same data is shown in this table with lines and shading.

Last	First	Address	City
Britt	James	550 Pine Rd.	Cedar Falls
Richter	Kim	103 7th St. S	Mankato
Pauls	Joe	30 Park Ave.	Chaska

Tables are also useful as lists for storing and tracking information.

Charts

Like the idiom "a picture is worth a thousand words," a chart is a great way to share data visually. For example, this table has data for an increase in sales trends. But the data is much easier to see and understand when it is presented in a chart. The table below provides more information about the most common types of charts.

	Proofreading checklist	
![Column icon]	Column	Column charts are used when you want to compare different values vertically, side-by-side.
![Line icon]	Line	Line charts are used to illustrate trends. Each value is plotted as a point on the chart and is connected to other values by a line.
![Pie icon]	Pie	Pie charts are useful for showing values as a percentage of a whole. The values for each item are represented by different colors.
![Bar icon]	Bar	Bar charts are just like column charts, except they display information in horizontal bars rather than in vertical columns.
![Area icon]	Area	Area charts are the same as line charts, except the area beneath the lines are filled with color. This creates a 2D effect in the chart.
![Flowchart icon]	Flowchart	Flowcharts are used to show relationships and processes.

Travel Destinations

Of clients who purchased our Western Europe package, ten purchased for business, twelve purchased for pleasure, five purchased for other reasons. Of clients who purchased our Central Europe package, twelve purchased for business, fifteen purchased for pleasure, eight purchased for other reasons. Of clients who purchased our Eastern Europe package, seven purchased for business, eight purchased for pleasure, two purchased for other reasons. One client purchased a package for Northern Europe.

Data is very difficult to read and understand when it is presented as text.

Better

Travel Destinations

	Business	Pleasure	Other
Western	10	12	5
Central	12	15	8
Eastern	7	8	2
Northern	0	0	1

Data is easier to read in a table, but analysis is left to the reader.

Best

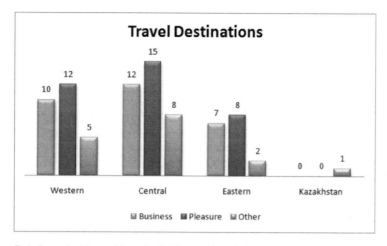

Data is easiest to read in a chart. Charts aid analysis by visually illustrating the data.

Unit 5

Letters, Memos, and E-mails

Letters, Memos, and E-mails – Introduction

Many business documents are written in the form of letters and memos. Both forms are similar in many regards, but the form that you choose will convey something about the tone and emotion of your message. Therefore, it is important to understand each form so your message is received as you hope for it to be. You'll learn more about letters and memos and how to use them correctly in this unit.

After we discuss letters and memos, we'll move on to e-mails. E-mail messages have steadily become the most common form of communication in business because it is flexible, versatile, and fast. Unfortunately, the very qualities that make e-mail user friendly also make it unbecoming of a business document. This unit will also discuss the proper use of e-mail messages as business documents.

Why Use a Letter?

Letters are the oldest and most formal type of business writing. Letters are an appropriate way to communicate with people outside your organization, such as clients or shareholders. Typically, a letter is written on your organization's stationery and is sent to an external audience. A letter can also be sent as an attachment to an e-mail. Here are a few hallmarks of the letter format:

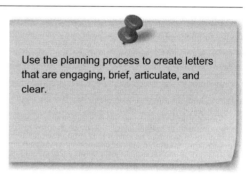

Use the planning process to create letters that are engaging, brief, articulate, and clear.

Conveys a message that is thoughtful, composed and articulate. Letters require good writing and composition. The message should be clear and organized, with good attention to detail.

Creates goodwill with the reader. Letters put the positive feelings of the reader in front of some of the guidelines for writing, such as brevity and directness. Letters aim to foster a positive relationship with the reader, no matter what information is included in the letter.

Anatomy of a Letter

All business letters have three major parts: introduction, body, and close. Surrounding these parts are elements that make up the business letter format. Use this lesson as a guide to the elements that make up a business letter.

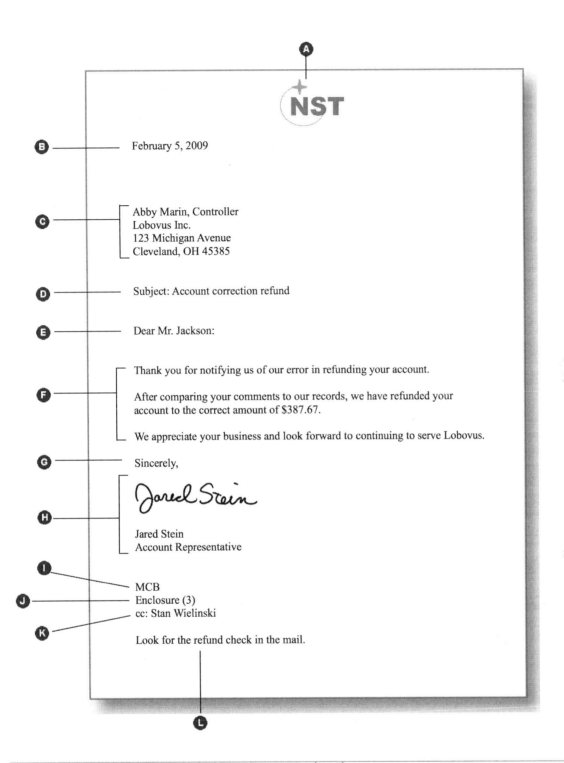

February 5, 2009

Abby Marin, Controller
Lobovus Inc.
123 Michigan Avenue
Cleveland, OH 45385

Subject: Account correction refund

Dear Mr. Jackson:

Thank you for notifying us of our error in refunding your account.

After comparing your comments to our records, we have refunded your account to the correct amount of $387.67.

We appreciate your business and look forward to continuing to serve Lobovus.

Sincerely,

Jared Stein
Account Representative

MCB
Enclosure (3)
cc: Stan Wielinski

Look for the refund check in the mail.

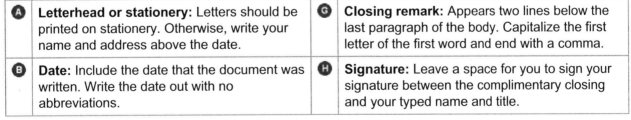

A	**Letterhead or stationery:** Letters should be printed on stationery. Otherwise, write your name and address above the date.	**G**	**Closing remark:** Appears two lines below the last paragraph of the body. Capitalize the first letter of the first word and end with a comma.
B	**Date:** Include the date that the document was written. Write the date out with no abbreviations.	**H**	**Signature:** Leave a space for you to sign your signature between the complimentary closing and your typed name and title.

C	**Recipient name and address:** Start with the recipient's name and title. Move the title to the line below the name if it is too long.	**I**	**Reference initials:** If someone other than the author typed the letter, include their initials here. Place them at the left margin, two lines below the signature line.
D	**Subject line (Optional):** This states the key issue of the letter so the reader knows what you are writing about right away. You may choose to use it when responding to a letter you have received. Some organizations use RE: for the subject line, which is short for regarding.	**J**	**Enclosure notation:** Incude an enclosure notation when you are enclosing something in the envelope. There are many variations on how to do this. In this example, there are three items in the envelope, For your own use, follow your organization's standards, or use whatever variation seems most clear to you. Place at the left margin two lines below the signature line, or directly below the reference initials.
E	**Salutation:** This is a greeting to the recipient. Address the recipent by their first name—Dear Fred,—only if you are on first-name basis. Avoid using "To whom it may concern:" as a salutation. Find out the person's name if you can, or refer to the recipient by his or her title, such as "Dear Customer Service Rep."	**K**	**Courtesy copy:** The copy notation (cc:) lists other people who will receive a copy of the letter. Also sometimes referred to as carbon copy. These recipients are different from the letter recipient(s) because action is not required of them.
F	**Body:** Single space paragraphs in the body, and double space between paragraphs. Even if they are all in one paragraph, the body should have three parts: introduction, supporting points, closing. **Introduction:** Begin with an introduction that tells teh reader the purpose of the letter and sets the tone of the letter. Make the key issue prominent. **Supporting points:** Follow the introduction with one or more paragraphs that support the key issue. **Closing:** Summarize or repeat the key issue of the document in the last paragraph of the body.	**L**	**Postscript:** Use this to emphasize a point, or call attention to something. Studies show this is the second-most read section of the letter. Postscripts are best for mass mailings. If you use a postscript too often in regular correspondence, its impact is often diminished.

I. MATCHING.
Match the correct term to the definition.

1. ____ leave a space for this between the complimentary closing and your typed name and title

2. ____ start with this, after the date

3. ____ use this to emphasize a point or call attention to something

4. ____ contains single spaced paragraphs and double spaces between paragraphs

5. ____ lists other people who will receive a copy of the letter

6. ____ write out with no abbreviation; first line of the letter

7. ____ greeting to the recipient

8. ____ use this when you are enclosing something in the envelope

9. ____ states the key issue of the letter

10. ____ appears two lines below the last paragraph of the body

11. ____ include their initials if someone other than the author typed the letter

12. ____ print letters on this

A. reference initials
B. signature
C. courtesy copy
D. recipient name and address
E. enclosure notation
F. closing remark
G. body
H. salutation
I. postscript
J. subject line
K. stationery
L. date

Letter Styles

Business letters are a formal style of writing, so you should follow a formal letter format. Choose the layout that works best for you and the message of your letter, or follow the layout that is preferred by your organization.

[Your address (if no stationery with letterhead)]
[Date]

4 lines

[Recipient name, title]
[Company name]
[Address]
[Address]
1 line
[Salutation]
1 line
The full block layout is easy to remember and execute. Everything is aligned at the left margin, and body paragraphs are separated by one line.
1 line
This style of letter is formal, readable, and flexible.
1 line
[Closing remark]

4 lines

[Your name, title]
1 line
[Reference initials]
Enclosures: [Number]
Cc: [Name for copy]
1 line
[Postscript]

Full Block

[Date]
[Recipient name, title]
[Company name]
[Address]
[Address]

1 line

[Subject (optional)]

1 line

[Salutation]

1 line

Block format is also sometimes called modified block format. It is a pleasant variation from full block layout.

1 line

Some elements appear closer to the right margin, such as the date, recipient address, complimentary closing, and signature. Salutation, body paragraphs, and ending notations are aligned at the left margin, and paragraphs are separated by one line.

1 line

Use the <Tab> key to align items along the same indentation to the right.

1 line

[Closing remark]

4 lines

[Your name, title]

1 line

[Reference initials]
[Enclosure]
[Courtesy copy]

1 line

[Postscript]

Block

[Date]
[Recipient name, title]
[Company name]
[Address]
[Address]
1 line
[Subject (optional)]
1 line
[Salutation]
1 line

This is just like block format, where items in the format are aligned similarly. The difference is that the first line of each paragraph is indented half an inch.
1 line

This format has more white space because of the indentation at the beginning of each paragraph.
1 line

[Closing remark]

4 lines

[Your name, title]
1 line
[Reference initials]
[Enclosure]
[Courtesy copy]
1 line
[Postscript]

Semiblock

I. MULTIPLE CHOICE.
Choose the best answer.

1. In the Block letter, the salutation comes after _____.
   - ○ the reference initials
   - ○ your name, title
   - ○ the subject
   - ○ the body

2. Your name and title preceed the reference initials in the _____ letter.
   - ○ Full block
   - ○ Block
   - ○ Semiblock
   - ○ all of the above

3. If you don't have stationery with letterhead, include your address before the date in the _____ letter.
   - ○ Full block
   - ○ Block
   - ○ Semiblock
   - ○ all of the above

4. The first line of each paragraph is indented half an inch in the _____ letter.
   - ○ Full block
   - ○ Block
   - ○ Semiblock
   - ○ all of the above

5. The courtesy copy name comes right before the _____ in all three letter styles.
   - ○ enclosure
   - ○ postscript
   - ○ closing remark
   - ○ body

Multiple Page Letters

Business letters usually fit on just one page. If they go beyond that, use these formatting tips for the extra pages.

Formatting for multiple pages

For letters that require extra pages, follow these guidelines:

Include the page number in the top left. Here are a few ways to include this information:

> Page 2
> Page 2 of 5
> 2

Use the same page number format on all pages.

Use plain white paper. Your organization's stationery or letterhead should be used for the first page. Any pages beyond the first page should be plain white paper, unless otherwise directed.

Page 2

You may also add recipient name, date, and subject line above the page number:

Include the closing elements, such as complimentary close and signature, at the end of the last page, just as you would at the end of a one-page letter.

Sincerely,

[Signature]

[Your name, title]

[Reference initials]
[Enclosure]
[Courtesy copy]

Use headings. Headings aid readers in long documents. They mark related paragraphs, making the topics in the document easy to scan. Headings provide a map of the document to the reader, and help you organize and write the document.

Keep related headings and paragraphs together. Headings should appear directly above related paragraphs. Don't allow a heading to be stranded from related paragraphs.

Don't allow orphans or widows. Orphans and widows are stray lines of paragraphs. Many word processors automatically prevent this from happening, but check for this in your proofreading as well.

Keep it to one page

If your letter just barely spills over onto the second page, there are a few tricks you can do to get your letter back to one page.

Orphan

Orphans and widows are typesetting terms for lines that are separated from the rest of a paragraph. An orphan is a paragraph-opening line that appears by itself at the bottom of a page or column. It can also be a word, part of a word, or a very short line that appears by itself at the end of a paragraph.

A mnemonic device to

1

remember the terms, is that "an orphan has no past; a widow has no future."

2

Widow

Orphans and widows are typesetting terms for lines that are separated from the rest of a paragraph.

A widow is a paragraph-ending line that falls at the beginning of the following page/column, thus separated from the remainder of the text. Widows happen last; they appear at the "death" (end) of

1

paragraphs.

2

Decrease the size of the font. This will fit more words on the page, but don't make the text so small that it is unreadable.

Decrease the size of the margins. This will allow more text to fit on the page.

Use the Shrink to One Page command. Preview the letter in Microsoft Word. Click the Shrink to One page button on the Preview toolbar.

I. **FILL IN THE BLANK.**
   Enter the correct word in the blank provided.

1. _____ mark related paragraphs, making the topics in the document easy to scan.

2. To make more words fit on the page, _____ the size of the font without making it too small to read.

3. Include the page number in the _____ of the page.

4. Business letters usually fit on _____ page.

Why Use a Memo?

Memos are an efficient and effective way to communicate between people in an organization. They typically are only one page long, are not detailed, and are sent to multiple people in paper or e-mail format. The primary purpose of a memo is to share information quickly and concisely. Memos can be used for any kind of office communication, such as to make an announcement, serve as a reminder, deliver a proposal, call a meeting, and so forth. Here are a few hallmarks of the memo format:

The content is easy to read. Memos are read very quickly. Readers should be able to scan the first few lines and paragraphs and know what the memo is about.

The writing is brief, clear, and direct. Writing this way ensures the memo is easy to read and understand. Keep a memo to one or two subjects so that a response is quick and easy.

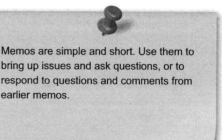

Memos are simple and short. Use them to bring up issues and ask questions, or to respond to questions and comments from earlier memos.

Key issue is easy to understand and remember. Get to the heart of the message in one or two sentences. Use expressive writing to make your message stand out.

Here are some common memo topics that you may find yourself writing about regularly:

- announce a meeting
- set a meeting agenda
- request action
- respond to a memo
- share new policy information

Anatomy of a Memo

The format of a memo is designed to make information easy to access and scan. Most organizations have their own memo form, but you can use this lesson as a guide to the most common elements of a business memo.

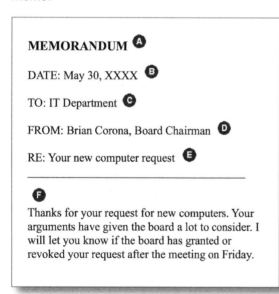

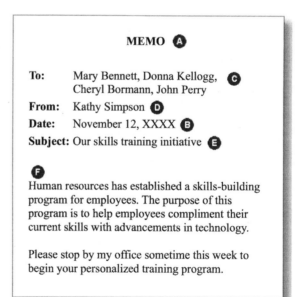

	Memorandum or Memo: This often appears at the top of a memo so the document is immediately identifiable to readers.
	Date: Write out the date that the memo is sent.

C	**To:** Include the names of people who will receive the memo. In some cases, include their titles so others know why they are included on the memo. You may also refer to the name of a department, if all people in the department or team are to receive the memo. Follow in-house guidelines in both cases.
D	**From:** State your name. Include your title if necessary, such as to communicate the calidity or relevance of your message. Include the names of others if they are involved in writing or sending the memo.
E	**Subject or Re:** Write the key issue of the memo here. The subject should be very clear and specific. This makes the memo easier to file and find later, and it also helps readers absorb the message of the memo. A helpful way to fill in the subject line is to complete this statement: "I am writing this memo to tell people about _____."
F	**Body:** Expand on the subject briefly. Many memos begin by acknowledging the purpose of the memo followed with a discussion of the subject, and end with a summary of the discussion.

I. **MULTIPLE CHOICE.**
   Choose the best answer.

1. The word (◯To, ◯Memorandum) often appears at the top of a memo so the document is immediately identifiable to readers.

2. The (◯body, ◯subject) is for expanding on the subject briefly.

3. When you state your name and your title, it belongs on the (◯RE:, ◯FROM:) line.

Why Use E-mail?

E-mail is a rapid and efficient mode of communication. Messages are sent and received in the blink of an eye, saving time, paper, and postage costs. E-mail messages are usually simple and short. They read like a conversation with immediate send and response turnaround. A letter is more like listening to someone talk, like a lecture or speech. It is no wonder e-mail has rapidly become the primary form of writing in business. Hallmarks of the e-mail format include:

- Instant communication. E-mails are delivered instantly, and can usually be read at a glance.
- Quick, brief messages. Messages are short and to the point.
- Flexibility. Messages can be formal or informal. They can be sent to one or one thousand people. Attachments provide a way to send long documents and additional information.
- Easy to file. E-mail messages are easy to store and save until they are needed.
- Time saving and cost effective. E-mail messages save time because they are sent immediately, and because they are

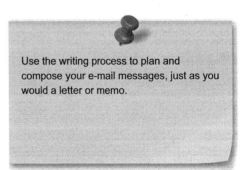
Use the writing process to plan and compose your e-mail messages, just as you would a letter or memo.

easy to write, send, and read. They are cost effective because they are no paper or postage costs.

Here are some common memo topics that you may find yourself writing about regularly:

- ask a colleague a question
- inform a client of their renewal date
- share meeting minutes
- topics for which you would use a memo

It is also very common for administrative assistants to manage more than one e-mail account. You may need to check your own e-mail, your direct manager's, and general inquiry inboxes. For example, your company might have an info@yourcompany.com box where customers can request pricing or product information. In that situation, you would check that e-mail inbox several times a day and reply to any questions. If you help your boss manage his or her inbox, you may need to frequently scan through the messages and sort out the items needing immediate attention. Occasionally, you may also be authorized to reply to messages for your manager. Remember to use professional languauge in every e-mail!

Anatomy of an E-mail Message

The format of an e-mail is similar to a memo, making information easy to access and scan. Though the arrangement varies, most e-mail programs include the same items in an e-mail message form.

To: jtrudeau@acme.com **Ⓐ**
Cc: lmoore@acme.com **Ⓑ**
Subject: Friday meeting agenda **Ⓒ**
Attachment: Marketing.doc **Ⓓ**

Ⓔ
Hi Jeanne,

Here is the agenda you requested for the meeting on Friday. The marketing document is a supplement for attendees to read beforehand and bring with them. Please confirm the agenda before Thursday.

Regards,

Reed

Reed Stephens | Account Manager **Ⓕ**
North Shore Travel
Office: 402-651-1234
rstephe@nst.com

A	**To:** Include the e-mail addresses of everyone for whom the message is intended. These are people that you expect to reply to you or to take action based on your e-mail.
B	**Cc or Bcc:** Send a courtesy copy (Cc) to users by adding their e-mail address in this line. These are recipients who don't need to reply or take action, but you still want to keep them informed. All recipients can see who has received a Cc copy of the message. The Bcc field stands for blind courtesy copy. Use this to share the message with someone without the other recipients knowing. Recipients in the To and Cc lines cannot see who has received a Bcc copy of the message.
C	**Subject:** Write the key issue of the e-mail here. The subject should be informative so that recipients know what the message is about before opening it, and interesting so that they want to open it. The subject should be very clear and specific. This makes the email easier to file and find later, and it also helps readers absorb the message of the e-mail. A helpful way to fill in the subject line is to complete this statement: "I am writing this e-mail to tell people about _____." Always enter something int he subject of the message. Recipients are less likely to read a message without text in the subject.
D	**Attachment:** Add files and documents to be sent with the e-mail message.

I. TRUE/FALSE.
Mark the following true or false.

1. Attachments are files and documents to be sent with an e-mail message.
   - ○ true
   - ○ false

2. Only include a signature at the end of a message if you do not know the recipient personally.
   - ○ true
   - ○ false

3. The key issue of an e-mail should be written in the Bcc: line.
   - ○ true
   - ○ false

4. Include the e-mail addresses of everyone for whom the message is intended in the To: line.
   - ○ true
   - ○ false

E-mail Dos and Don'ts

E-mail is an important form of business communication. Take the time to plan, compose, and edit your e-mail messages, even if the process is very brief, giving them the same care and attention that you would a longer type of document. Follow these guidelines to make your e-mail messages more effective and energetic.

E-mail Dos	
Put the key issue in the subject line.	The subject line tells the reader what your message is about. Make it short, specific, and to the point.
Keep the message short.	Try to make the content of your message fit on one screen. Use an attachment or another document if you need to send a lot of information.
Remember that e-mails are on the record.	E-mail messages can be used in disciplinary or judicial procedures, so don't e-mail anything that could be used against you later. Deleting a message doesn't make you safe; deleted messages are stored on your organization's e-mail servers even after the message has been deleted from your inbox.
Double-check the address in the To, Cc, and Bcc fields.	Make sure the message is being sent to the right people.
Keep personal messages separate from work messages.	Keep personal communication in a separate e-mail account so that you don't have to spend work time on personal matters.

Be professional.	Part of the convenience of e-mail is that it is easy to write and it has a more conversational tone than letters and memos. However, you still need to maintain a professional and polished image.
Include your signature at the end of the message.	Business e-mails include a signature that shares the name of the sender along with their contact information. This is standard procedure. Follow your organization's e-mail policy to determine the correct construction of your signature.
Include a brief greeting.	E-mail is informal, but including a greeting before diving into your message is a courtesy.
Use correct punctuation.	This includes using capital letters at the beginning of sentences and proper nouns, adding periods to the end of sentences, and organizing content into paragraphs.

E-mail Don'ts	
Write unnecessary messages.	E-mail messages are so easy to write and send that people sometimes send unnecessary messages that waste time—such as a humorous forwards, confirming confirmations, and a thank you for a thank you.
Send without editing and re-reading your message.	Though it's not uncommon to see e-mail messages with typos, misspellings, and poor grammar, such errors are unacceptable in business writing. Edit your messages so words are spelled correctly, letters are capitalized, correct punctuation is used, and the message is clear.
Send messages when you are emotional.	Wait at least one hour to calm down, and then edit the message. When your message is clear and rational, send it on.
Offend colleagues with forwards and questionable message content.	Avoid political and religious topics and racy forwards. Be professional with your message content.
Substitute e-mail for face-to-face conversation.	Because it is such an immediate form of communication, some people feel e-mail is an acceptable substitute for conversation. It isn't. Don't hide behind your e-mail messages and use them to avoid a stressful encounter.
Use all caps.	DO NOT USE ALL CAPS IN YOUR MESSAGES. ALL CAPS MEANS SHOUTING. You do not want to shout at your business associates, especially your boss or clients.

I. MATCHING.
Determine whether the following sentences are E-mail Dos or Don'ts.

1. ____ Use all caps.

2. ____ Send messages when you are emotional.

3. ____ Be professional.

4. ____ Write unnecessary messages.

5. ____ Include a brief greeting.

6. ____ Keep the message short.

7. ____ Put the key issue in the subject line.

8. ____ Substitute e-mail for face to face conversation.

A. E-mail Do

B. E-mail Don't

Unit 6
Writing Templates

Writing Templates – Introduction

So you understand the planning process of writing, you understand the importance of tone and word choice, but you're still having trouble writing your documents. Look no further: these writing templates are great guidelines for writing business documents.

Use the writing templates in this chapter for all of your writing needs. Just identify the type of document that you wish to write, for example one that shares good news, look up the writing template, and fill in your own information. Be prepared to refer back to this chapter frequently, or at least until you have the templates you use most often memorized.

Requests for Information

Asking for information is very straightforward, and it's something that you probably do a lot. Your job is to make sure your request is clearly understood.

> **Question:** Ask specifically for the information you want. If you can put this in a question form, it will help indicate to the reader that you want them to answer your question.

> **Explanation (Optional):** Give a background explanation of why you need the information.

> **List of Questions (Optional):** Break your request into a list of specific questions. This will make it easier for the reader to respond to your questions.

> **Friendly Ending:** A friendly ending will close the request in a positive light, leaving a good impression on the reader.

Use this formula when you need to:

- Ask for information about a product or service. For example, if you have questions on the pricing model for a service.
- Ask someone a question, or ask them to do something. For example, you've read a report of a colleague and have questions on some of the data, or you want them to send another version of a chart.

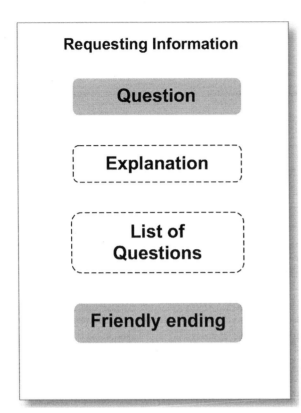

Requesting Information	Example
Question	Dear Zoning Committee,
Explanation	What are the zoning laws for business buildings in our city?
List of Questions	My company purchased a new office building and we would like to make internal and external changes. We are especially interested in information regarding these matters:
Friendly ending	• Restrictions on outdoor decks. • Restrictions on basement facilities. Thanks in advance for your prompt reply. We are anxious to begin remodeling. Sincerely, David Galbraith

Dashed outlines indicate optional paragraphs.

Requests to Fix a Problem

Asking your reader to fix a problem takes some finesse. Your request should be phrased in a way that will make them receptive to your situation and eager to help you.

State the problem: Begin by stating the problem you're experiencing. This makes the reader feel invited to help you solve the problem, rather than blamed for the problem.

Give background information: Provide background information describing the problem.

Offer a remedy to the problem: Help your reader meet your expectations by offering solutions that would meet your standards.

Friendly ending: A friendly ending will close the request in a positive light, leaving a good impression on the reader.

Use this formula when you need to:

- Ask someone to fix a problem; to register a complaint. For example, if you have a problem with a product made by the company.
- Tell someone you've made a mistake, and that you're going to fix it. For example, you've found an error with an order a client has made, and you want to notify them that you're aware of the error and you want them to know how you're going to fix it.

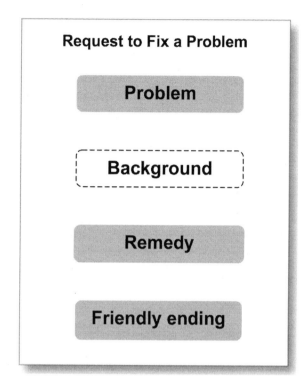

Request to Fix a Problem	Example
Problem	Dear ACME Paper: There was a problem with the paper you supplied to our company last week.
Background	Our shipment arrived on time, but our employees found that the letterhead that appeared at the top of the stationery was incorrect.
Remedy	Will you please send us a new shipment of stationery with the correct letterhead? We will also accept a full refund of the order.
Friendly ending	Thanks in advance for resolving this matter. Sincerely,

Dashed outlines indicate optional paragraphs.

Delivering Good News

Good news is one of the easiest communications to write, because the message is already positive, and the reader is very receptive to what you have to say.

Start with the good news: Begin with a positive word, such as "yes" or "you," so the reader immediately knows what to expect.

Explain or qualify the good news: State the reason the individual(s) is receiving the good news, or any background information that is necessary.

Friendly Ending: A friendly ending will close the letter in a positive light, leaving a good impression on the reader.

Use this formula when you need to:

- Recognize someone for a job well done.
- Notify someone of acceptance into a program or school.
- Offer a job to someone.
- Thank someone.

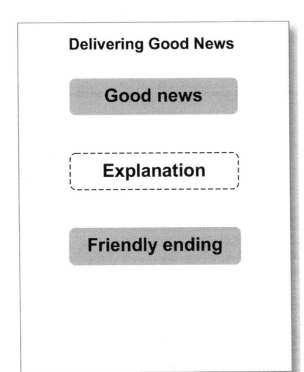

Delivering Good News	Example
Good news	Dear Mrs. Green:
Explanation	Congratulations! You have been accepted to our three-day seminar, "Advertising and the Internet."
Friendly ending	You are one of 50 applicants that has been chosen for the seminar. Please see the enclosed documents for more information on the seminar.

Dashed outlines indicate optional paragraphs.

Delivering Bad News

Bad news is a very difficult type of message to write, because no one wants to read bad news. When your audience is naturally closed to your message, your job as a writer is more difficult.

Acknowledgement: Begin with a neutral statement that establishes context for the message.

Background: Provide information about how the bad news came about, such as how the decision was reached, or the events that transpired.

Bad news: State the bad news. The reader should be prepared for this since the context and background has already been established. Follow this with a positive statement.

Friendly ending: Close with a friendly ending to leave the reader with a positive thought.

Use this template when you need to:

- Collect payment on a bill.
- Notify someone of rejection from a program or school.

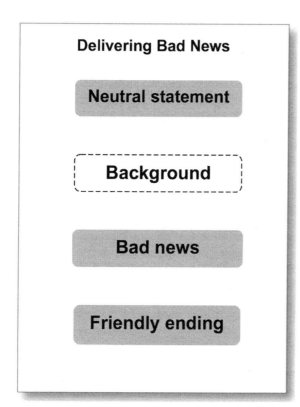

Delivering Bad News	Example
Neutral statement	Dear Mr. Danielson:
Background	Thank you for your request for a credit increase. We appreciate the opportunity to serve you.
Bad news	We have reviewed your application and your credit history with us and the credit bureau.
Friendly ending	Unfortunately, we are unable to grant your request at this time.

Dashed outlines indicate optional paragraphs.

Direct Persuasion

Persuasion is one of the most difficult types of communication. It is an essential skill, however, because effective leaders have the ability to change minds. This form of persuasion assumes your audience is open to your point of view and can be persuaded by good logic.

State your position: State the issue at hand and your opinion: the key issue.

State your reasons: Explain why you feel this way. Persuade your readers with facts and logic, and emotion when appropriate.

Repeat your position and friendly ending: Close the letter stating your position once again, and add a personal ending.

Use this template when you need to:

- Persuade colleagues to your point of view.
- Persuade a client to buy your product.
- Write a letter of recommendation.

Direct Persuasion	Example
Your position	Dear Mr. Patel:
	Thank you for your interest in the school bus company for our school district.
Reasoning	I support our school board in their decision to sign a contract with a national bus company over the local company.
Your position with friendly ending	This is the right decision because it will save our district money that is needed for other programs. For example, the savings are enough to keep our language and arts classes. Our children won't be getting a quality education without these well-rounded, cultural classes.
	The decision to save money and go with the national vendor will pay off in the quality of education our school district is able to provide.
	Sincerely,
	Jennie Bonderman
	Jennie Bonderman

Indirect Persuasion

In cases where you might have a harder time convincing people of your point of view, use indirect persuasion. This persuasion is more complex. It understands that the audience is not willing to give up their position, regardless of the logic and reasoning presented. To persuade them, you need to create an atmosphere of cooperation and mutual understanding. When you show that you can see from their point of view, they will be more open to seeing yours.

State the problem objectively: This puts you and the reader on even ground. No point of view is advocated at this point: you are on equal terms.

State the opposing position and reasoning: Gives you an impression of fairness, that you are fair and reasonable, and that you can understand their point of view. This tips the argument in their favor.

State your position and reasoning: State your views in a way that tips the argument back to equal terms.

Describe why your perspective is right: Once you have established rapport with the readers, explain why your position is the right one. You may further goodwill with the reader by suggesting that their position may be the right one, but at another time and in another situation.

Repeat your position and closing: Remind the reader of your position and end the letter on a personal note.

Use this template when you need to:

- Persuade colleagues to your point of view.
- Do a lot of persuading.

Indirect Persuasion

Problem at hand

Opposing view
and reasoning

Your position
and reasoning

Why your position
is right

Your position with
friendly ending

Example

Dear Mr. Patel:

Thank you for your interest in the school board's upcoming vote on the bus company. Our school board has a difficult decision ahead of them as they decide which bus company to hire.

While the cost is higher, signing a contract with our local bus company will support local business and keep taxpayer dollars in the community.

On the other hand, we can save the district money by hiring a larger national company. Those savings can then be put toward valuable programs, such as languages and the arts.

Therefore, I support the decision to save money and hire the national company to do our bussing for the next academic year. Providing quality education is the highest priority for our school district, and language and arts classes are an essential component of a well-rounded education. If cut these important cultural programs, it will be extremely difficult to get them back.

Sincerely

Jennie Bonderman

Jennie Bonderman

Answer Key

Before You Start Writing

Getting Started

I. MATCHING.

1. D. audience
2. B. key issue
3. A. delivery
4. C. objective

Who is Your Audience?

I. FILL IN THE BLANK.

1. positive
2. needs
3. adjust
4. benefit
5. visuals

What is the Best Way to Deliver Your Message?

I. MULTIPLE CHOICE.

1. Letter
2. Memo
3. E-mail
4. Letter
5. E-mail

What to Say and How to Say It

Getting Your Thoughts Organized

I. TRUE/FALSE.

1. false
2. true
3. false

Anatomy of Communication

I. FILL IN THE BLANK.

1. body
2. summary
3. set the tone
4. key issue

Writing Paragraphs and Sentences

I. MULTIPLE CHOICE.

1. Each paragraph contains only one subject, verb, and object.
2. the person or thing
3. You can do any of the above to vary the structure of a sentence.

Write the Right Way

I. TRUE/FALSE.
1. true
2. false
3. false
4. true
5. false

Be Clear

I. FILL IN THE BLANK.
1. definite
2. passive filler
3. acronyms

Be Active

I. MATCHING.
1. A. active
2. B. passive
3. A. active
4. B. passive
5. B. passive

Be Professional

I. MATCHING.
1. A. gender neutral
2. B. gender biased
3. A. gender neutral
4. A. gender neutral
5. B. gender biased
6. A. gender neutral
7. B. gender biased
8. B. gender biased

Editing and Design

Preparing to Edit

I. FILL IN THE BLANK.
1. white space
2. silently
3. angry
4. feedback

Font Formatting

I. TRUE/FALSE.
1. false
2. true
3. true

Paragraph Formatting

I. MULTIPLE CHOICE.
1. five
2. Numbered
3. margins
4. White space

Letters, Memos, and E-mails

Anatomy of a Letter

I. MATCHING.

1. B. signature
2. D. recipient name and address
3. I. postscript
4. G. body
5. C. courtesy copy
6. L. date
7. H. salutation
8. E. enclosure notation
9. J. subject line
10. F. closing remark
11. A. reference initials
12. K. stationery

Letter Styles

I. MULTIPLE CHOICE.

1. the subject
2. all of the above
3. Full block
4. Semiblock
5. postscript

Multiple Page Letters

I. FILL IN THE BLANK.

1. Headings
2. decrease
3. top left
4. one

Anatomy of a Memo

I. MULTIPLE CHOICE.

1. Memorandum
2. body
3. FROM:

Anatomy of an E-mail Message

I. TRUE/FALSE.

1. true
2. false
3. false
4. true

E-mail Dos and Don'ts

I. MATCHING.

1. B. E-mail Don't
2. B. E-mail Don't
3. A. E-mail Do
4. B. E-mail Don't
5. A. E-mail Do
6. A. E-mail Do
7. A. E-mail Do
8. B. E-mail Don't